THE LIFE-CHANGING MAGIC OF
SKATEBOARDING

A BEGINNER'S GUIDE
WITH OLYMPIC MEDALIST SKY BROWN

BY

SKY BROWN

MAGIC CAT 🐱 PUBLISHING

NEW YORK

HI, I'M SKY BROWN.

I'm here to tell you about how skateboarding
changed my life . . . and share the magic
of it with you too.

I WAS TWO, MAYBE THREE YEARS OLD

when I started skateboarding. I was really small,
but I knew I loved it, even then.

My dad would skate every day
on a ramp he'd built in our backyard,
and he would push me around on my
little board too.

It was so much fun.

I would go everywhere I could
with that little skateboard.
It was my favorite toy!

GUESS WHAT?

I'm going to be talking about the board all the time in this book, so let's just have a quick look at one together.

Here are the names of all the parts of a skateboard:

The **DECK** is the wooden part of the board that you stand on.

NUTS, BOLTS, AND SCREWS hold the trucks onto the board.

The **TRUCKS** connect the wheels to the board.

WHEELS are what you move on!

ELBOW PADS

Here's what I wear when I skate:

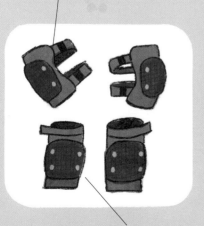

KNEE PADS

HELMET

SNEAKERS

Skateboards come in all sorts of designs too. You can choose your favorite colors, or even customize one that is unique to you!

classic

old school

carving longboard

cruiser

pintail

downhill

twin tip

They can be different shapes and sizes, depending on what kind of skating you are doing.

And how **big** your feet are!

WHEN I WAS EIGHT, I convinced my mom and dad to let me enter my first competition.

It was a big contest that would be on TV. I was the youngest skater ever to compete!

When it was my turn to skate, I just dropped into my run and had the best time.

I couldn't stop smiling. I was so stoked to be there.

After I landed one of my big tricks, the announcer said,
"Half of the pro guys here can't do that!"
That made me smile even wider.

I loved competing, and I wanted to do more of it.

When I turned ten, I became a professional skater—the youngest professional skateboarder in the world. I was an Olympic medalist by the age of thirteen and a world champion at fourteen!

So—let me tell you how I got here, and how you can learn to skate like me too!

#1 TAKE BABY STEPS TO START

After I got my first skateboard, I needed to get comfortable and feel how it moved.

Once I was ready, I got used to standing up on the board.

That's when I worked out which of my feet felt most comfortable at the front of the board.

If your left foot feels better in the front, you have a **regular stance**.

If your right foot feels more comfortable at the front, you have a **goofy stance**, like me!

I practiced standing for a while, on soft surfaces like grass or carpet, so it wouldn't hurt too much if I fell off.

Once my stride got longer, I could place my back foot on the board while I was riding along. I had to practice hard to get all these things right at the start.

See how this **regular** skater's foot turns a little so it's pointing in the same direction as their back foot?

Every time they take their back foot off to push, they shift their front foot a little so it's facing forward again.

Then, they lean their weight into their toes or their heels. Their skateboard's **trucks** will follow the direction of their lean, and they'll gradually turn.

#2 LEARN TO STOP AS WELL AS GO!

Once I got moving, I needed to know how to stop!

There's two ways I learned to do it. Here's my **regular stance** friend again to show you how. You'll need to practice a lot to get good at stopping.

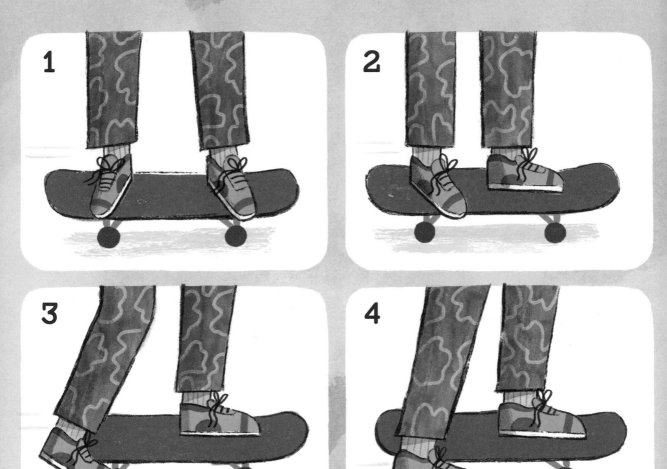

1

2

3

4

Foot brake
Put your back foot on the ground and
let it drag along until you come to a stop.

Tail scrape
Put your weight on the tail of your board
so the nose tips up.

1

2

3

TAIL

NOSE

The tail will drag along the ground, slowing you down.

Practice the tipping movement on soft ground first. Then, once
you're really confident, you can try it while you're riding.

Both methods
might cause some wear and tear
to your board or your shoes, so
just check with your grown-up
that this is okay!

In skateboarding, we don't train the way athletes in other sports do.

I don't go to the same place to practice for a certain number of hours.
I don't have a coach, either.

I *do* skate every day, though.

Some days I might work on a new trick.

If I'm preparing for a competition I might practice my tricks a few times, to get them looking clean and stylish.

And sometimes I might just go cruising with my dad and my little brother, Ocean. We love to skate at the beach at sunset.

Whatever I am doing, all that really matters is that I am spending time on my skateboard and having **FUN**.

#4 DO OTHER THINGS THAT MAKE YOU HAPPY

Skateboarding means so much to me, but there are other things that I enjoy too, like surfing and fashion.

In 2018, I was offered the chance to do something so rad I couldn't say no. But it was nothing to do with skateboarding . . .

It was *Dancing with the Stars: Juniors!*

I was *so* scared to try dancing . . .

. . . but I also had the same excited feeling I get when I dare myself to do a new trick.

I started my first dance riding in on my skateboard.

Eight weeks later, I won the whole season with my partner, JT.

AND I got to wear some awesome dance costumes too! I was so happy.

DWTSJ helped me learn to face my fear and do a scary thing anyway. It still helps me now, even though I've swapped my dancing shoes back to skate shoes.

CHOOSE YOUR OWN JOURNEY

When skateboarders compete, we make up our own runs.

We choose the tricks we perform and the line we skate.
We get to choose the journey we take around the bowl.
Every bowl is different, so every skater will skate it in a different way.

When I drop into a bowl, which is full of curves and obstacles to flow around, I don't always know the line I'm going to skate.

The sides of the bowl are steep so we can work up speed to do our tricks high in the air.

But that's okay. I love feeling my way around somewhere new.

I always try and make my tricks as beautiful and powerful and high as I can. That's my style and my choice.

DROPPING IN

For your first drop-in, position your skateboard at the edge of the bowl and put your back foot on the tail so the board's nose is in the air.

Put your front foot onto or near the front truck bolts, lean your weight forward, and let yourself roll.

It'll be scary the first time, but try and relax into it!

My helmet saved my life when I fell.

In 2020, I was practicing a trick on a really high ramp.

Before I could do anything about it, I was going off the edge of the ramp.

I fell a long way.

I don't remember anything else.

I woke up in the hospital.

I had fractured my skull, my arm, and some of my fingers. I was lucky to be alive . . .

and grateful for my gear.

There's lots of safety gear you can wear to protect yourself when you skate.

Wrist guards help to strengthen the delicate bones in your wrists. I wore a wrist guard for a while after my fall.

Make sure a new **helmet** fits you properly. A skate shop will help you find the perfect helmet for you.

Pads help protect you from bumps and scrapes. **Knee pads** are really useful as you can slide down a ramp on your knees if you need to bail out of a trick.

Your shoes should have a **flat** sole with plenty of grip.

START WITH AN OLLIE

Skaters love doing tricks! My first trick was an **ollie**.

An ollie is a rad trick to get really good at because some of the more difficult tricks build on what you do in an ollie.

1

When you're rolling at a speed that you're happy with, first make sure your front foot is just behind the front bolts.

2

Crouch low on the board.

3

Quickly push down on your back foot and jump up from that foot into the air.

4

Slide your front foot toward the nose of your board as you jump. Your board should lift with you. Both knees will be bending toward your chest.

5

Put a bit of weight into your front foot to balance out the board in the air so it's level.

6

Land with your knees bent and roll out.

To start with, you can practice these movements without rolling while you get used to doing things in the right order.

#8 EVERYONE FALLS SOMETIMES

After my big fall, I knew I just wanted to get back up and push even harder.

I knew that all skaters fall sometimes—that's just part of what we do. What really matters is that you get up and try again.

After two weeks, I did the first trick since my accident.

I had a cast on my arm, but being back on my board felt so good.

Here's a trick you can try on the flat ground—or on a ramp, if you feel ready!

Here's how to perform a **kick turn.**
This trick is a rad way to change direction!

1

Push off on your board, then turn your lead shoulder (it'll be the one on the same side as your front foot) slightly down and across your body, until it is past your hips.

2

Make sure your knees and ankles are bent and lean your weight forward, into your toes.

3

Push down a tiny bit on the tail with your back foot to create a slight lift of the nose, then turn your board in the same direction as your lead shoulder.

4

Land with your weight over your front foot and keep rolling. If it's over your back foot you might tip and fall off!

YOU'VE GOT THIS!

GO AS BIG AS YOU CAN!

Just over a year later, when I was thirteen, I competed in park at the X Games 2021.

I dropped into my first run and landed my **frontside 540**.

I had been the first girl ever to land it in competition, back when I was eleven!

People were starting to know me for that trick now, so it felt extra special to land it in this comp.

This is me in the middle of a frontside 540. It's an advanced trick that I had to work really hard on. Frontside means that I start off facing the ramp, and 540 means that I rotate one and a half times—or 540 degrees—in the air!

My first run was good enough to put me into the lead.

I had so many cool tricks in my bag that I could play around with and have fun.

I tried different things on each run. I took chances. It was totally sick.

I stayed in the lead and won the park event that day! But there was something even **MORE** incredible just waiting around the corner for me . . .

#10 DREAMS CAN COME TRUE

In 2021, I qualified for the Tokyo Olympics! I dreamed of how amazing it would be.

I would be representing Great Britain, where my dad was born, in Japan, where I was born.

And I would be the youngest person ever to compete for Team Great Britain in a Summer Olympics. So cool!

In my first run in Tokyo, I came off on my **kickflip indy**.

In my second run, I came off on . . . yep, you've guessed it! My kickflip indy. But I wasn't giving up. Nope.

In my third run, I gave it everything I had, and LANDED my kickflip indy! (I even finished up the run with a frontside 540. Rad!)

That final run snagged me the Olympic bronze medal in park. I was crying with happiness and, best of all, I got to skate the Olympics with all my friends. I had a total blast.

AND REMEMBER . . . DON'T GIVE UP! SOMETHING THAT GOES WRONG ONE DAY MIGHT GO RIGHT THE NEXT.

Even though my **kickflip indy** almost cost me an Olympic medal that day in Tokyo, I still LOVE doing it. And I'm never going to hate on a trick just because it doesn't go perfectly the first time!

Let me show you how to do this gnarly trick . . .

A kickflip indy is super difficult, so let's try a regular **kickflip** instead!

Remember the ollie from pages 20–21?
Well, a kickflip starts with the first part of that trick.

Do the first four steps of an ollie. Then, instead of leveling out the board, flick your front foot so it turns the nose of your board.

Keep your shoulders level.

28

If you're afraid to try, you'll miss out on how **AMAZING** it will feel when you succeed!

The **indy** part of a **kickflip indy** is when you grab the board with your hand before you put your feet back on the board and land.

3

Your board will turn a circle horizontally beneath you.

4

Get ready to land on both feet, with equal weight on your front and your back foot.

5

Roll away.

HOW SICK WAS THAT?!

BEFORE I GO,

I want to inspire kids like you to try the magic of skateboarding, and especially any girls that might be reading this.

There are still not enough girls skating, and I want to help change that.

I also want to help kids around the world living in difficult circumstances build their confidence and have fun by learning how to skateboard. Skating really can be **life-changing**.

Whenever people say I'm not enough, I want to prove them wrong.
I give it everything to show them that I can do it.

No matter what your dreams are for the future,
be brave, be strong, have fun, and, in everything you do . . .
DO IT 'CUZ YOU LOVE IT.

And if that's skateboarding, well, I'm **stoked** to hear it!

HOW TO . . . NOSE GRAB AND TAIL GRAB

When you're feeling good about your **ollie**, give these grabs a go!
You'll look rad at the skate park!

NOSE GRAB

1

Go into an ollie.

2

Let your front hand hang a bit lower than it usually would in an ollie.

3

Let the **nose** of your board come up to meet your hand, then grab the nose for a second!

4

Let the board go as you return to the ground and ride away!

TAIL GRAB

1

Go into a nice high ollie.
Try and work up a little bit of speed
to help, if you feel confident!

2

When you're in the air and you've
leveled out the board (see step **5** on
page 21), reach your back arm down.

3

Grab the **tail** of the board
and hold on for a second.

4

Let the board go as you return
to the ground and ride away!

HOW TO . . . FRONTSIDE 180

Remember my frontside 540? You might be able to do that too one day, but in the meantime, here's a version with less rotation called a **frontside 180** that you can practice a lot first.

1

In this trick, you are using your shoulders to help you move.

Go into an ollie, but just before you jump, start turning your shoulders frontside (toward your heels).

2

As you jump, because you're already halfway through the 180-degree turn with your shoulders, your hips and legs will follow in the same direction.

3

Bend your knees to land.

4

Roll away.

Because you'll have done a half turn, you're going to be landing **switch**. That means your feet are going to be in the opposite position to your normal stance on the board.

ALL ABOUT SKY

Sky Brown was born in Miyazaki, Japan on July 7, 2008. Her mom is Japanese and her dad is British. She has a little brother, Ocean.

Sky began skating and surfing at age two and quickly became famous when short videos of her gained millions of views on YouTube. She now lives in California.

Sky, age 11, and her brother, Ocean

Sky, age 7, surfing

Sky on a grind rail, age 6

Sky at the World Championships, age 14

Sky made history with her bronze medal win at the 2021 Tokyo Olympics, when she became Great Britain's youngest Summer Olympian. Sky is also the first female skater to land a frontside 540.

Sky, age 14, competing in the 2022 X Games

In July 2022, Sky won gold in the Women's Skateboard Park event at the X Games, the biggest worldwide skate competition. And in January 2023, Sky took gold in the World Championships.

Sky, age 14, at a skate park in Hawaii

Sky, age 10, and her partner, JT, performing on DWTSJ

In 2018, Sky also became the first-ever winner of the hit dance competition show, *Dancing with the Stars: Juniors*. When she's not skating, she loves surfing and spending time with friends.

Sky uses sports to help inspire young people around the world to follow their dreams and reach for their goals. She is a supporter of the international skateboarding charity Skateistan.

Sky, age 9, working with Skateistan

GLOSSARY

180: a half rotation

360: a full rotation

540: one and a half rotations!

Air: short for aerial; when you have all four wheels of your skateboard off the ground

Backside: when you're doing a trick and your back is facing the ramp

Bowl: a sunken area with high walls, obstacles, and curves to drop into and skate around

Deck: the flat body of your skateboard that you stand on

Drop in: when you enter a ramp or a bowl from the top

Frontside: when you're doing a trick and your front is facing the ramp

Grab: when you hold onto the board during an aerial trick

Goofy stance: if your right foot feels more comfortable at the front of the board

Indy: when you grab your board with your back hand between your feet while rotating backside

Kickflip: a trick that turns the board 360 degrees horizontally beneath you while you jump

Kickturn: when you lift and swing the nose of your board in a new direction

Ollie: a trick that pops the board into the air and you catch it with your feet

Nose: the front of your board

Ramp: a slope where you drop in from a high point and skate down to a lower point

Regular stance: if your left foot feels more comfortable at the front of the board

Run: a ride around a bowl and a series of tricks with a time limit in competitions

Tail: the back of your board

Trick: another name for a move

Trucks: connect your deck to your wheels and help you turn

This book is dedicated to Skateistan, a non-profit organization that uses skateboarding and education to empower children.
SB

For Dexter and Ottilie
SD

FURTHER READING

Girls on Wheels by Srividhya Venkat, illustrated by Kate Wadsworth

I've Got the No-Skateboard Blues by Anita Yasuda, illustrated by Jorge H. Santillan

Skateboard Tricks: Step by Step Instructions & Videos to Help You Land Your Next Trick! by Jack Boyd

There Goes Patti McGee!: The Story of the First Women's National Skateboard Champion by Tootie Nienow, illustrated by Erika Medina

The illustrations were created digitally.
Set in Calder and Vodka Sans.

Library of Congress Control Number 2023944460
ISBN 978-1-4197-7340-2

Text © 2024 Sky Brown
Illustrations © 2024 Shaw Davidson
Cover © 2024 Magic Cat
Book design by Stephanie Jones
Biography and cover images courtesy of Stu Brown, Getty Images, and Chris Dangaard

Printed and bound in China
10 9 8 7 6 5 4 3 2

Abrams books are available at special discounts when purchased in quantity for premiums and promotions as well as fundraising or educational use. as well as fundraising or educational use. Special editions can also be created to specification. For details, contact specialsales@abramsbooks.com or the address below.

MIX
Paper | Supporting responsible forestry
FSC® C144853

ABRAMS The Art of Books
195 Broadway, New York, NY 10007
abramsbooks.com